CHAPTER 1: **INTRODUCTION**

Hey there! I'm Paul, and let me tell you, I am pumped to share my transformative journey into the world of affiliate marketing with you. Get ready to buckle up, because we're going on a wild ride, diving deep into my experiences, the lessons I've learned, and how I turned my passion into a profitable online business that gave me the financial freedom I'd always dreamed of.

Before we dive into the nitty-gritty, let me share a bit about myself. I wasn't always this passionate entrepreneur, crushing it in the online space. No, I started as a regular guy, working a 9-to-5 job and feeling trapped in the rat race. Deep down, I knew there had to be more to life than merely grinding away for someone else's benefit. Today, I'm a full-time dad to two beautiful girls, and I can't emphasize enough how grateful I am to spend time with them every day, without worrying about the financial struggles that haunted me in the past.

One day, I stumbled upon the concept of high-ticket affiliate marketing. I was intrigued by the idea of earning passive income by promoting products I was genuinely passionate about. I mean, who wouldn't want to make money while they sleep? It felt like a no-brainer. So, I decided to take the plunge and dive headfirst into this new world of opportunities. I won't lie to you – the journey wasn't all sunshine and rainbows. I faced my fair share of challenges, setbacks, and failures along the way. But guess what? That's where the real learning happens. That's where you grow, adapt, and become the person you need to be to succeed in this game. Through trial and error, research, and connecting with other like-minded individuals, I started seeing progress. I began to learn the ins and outs of the industry, honing my skills and developing strategies that worked for me. And, ultimately, I discovered game-changing ways that took my affiliate marketing journey to new heights!

Now, I'm on a mission to share my knowledge, experience, and passion with you. My goal is to help you unlock your own potential, crush it in the world of affiliate marketing, and achieve the financial freedom you've always dreamed of. So, are you ready to hustle? Are you prepared to put in the work, be patient, and stay committed to your goals? If your answer is a resounding "YES", then let's get started, my friend. The path to success awaits, and I can't wait to see where this journey takes you!

CHAPTER 2: THE AFFILIATE MARKETING

Alright, my friend, it's time to dive headfirst into the incredible world of affiliate marketing! This chapter is all about laying the groundwork and making sure you understand the fundamentals of this game-changing business model. Trust me, once you grasp the concept and see the potential, there's no turning back.

So, what is affiliate marketing? At its core, affiliate marketing is a performance-based business model where you, as an affiliate, promote and recommend products or services to your audience. When someone purchases through your unique affiliate link, you earn a commission. It's a win-win situation: the company gets a sale, and you get a cut of the profits. Now, you might be thinking, "Okay, that sounds cool, but what's the big deal?" Well, let me tell you, the beauty of affiliate marketing lies in its scalability and passive income potential. With the right strategies, dedication, and persistence, you can build a thriving online business that generates income while you sleep, travel, or spend time with your family. Sounds pretty amazing, right?

To help you understand the affiliate marketing universe better, let's break it down into a few key components:

- The Niche: The first step in your affiliate marketing journey is to choose a niche. This is the specific market or industry you'll be focusing on. The key is to find something you're passionate about and genuinely interested in, as this will fuel your motivation and help you create valuable, engaging content for your audience. Whether it's health, fitness or cooking, it must be something that you love.
- The Affiliate Programs: Once you've chosen your niche, it's time to find relevant affiliate programs or networks.

These are the companies or platforms that offer affiliate partnerships and provide you with unique affiliate links to promote their products or services. Some popular networks include Amazon Associates, ClickBank, and ShareASale, just to name a few.

- The Platform: In order to promote your affiliate offers, you'll need a platform where you can connect with your target audience. This could be a blog, a YouTube channel, a podcast, or social media platforms like Instagram, Facebook, or TikTok. The key is to choose a platform that aligns with your strengths and interests, and where your target audience is most likely to be found. My tip? Try 'em all and find what works best with your niche.

- The Content: Now that you have your niche, your affiliate programs, and your platform, it's time to create killer content that educates, entertains, and engages your audience. This is where you'll showcase your expertise, build trust with your audience, and seamlessly promote your affiliate offers in a way that feels genuine and helpful. Bring value above all, don't ask to buy anything from you.

- The Promotion: Once you've created your content, it's time to promote it and drive traffic to your platform. This is where you'll leverage various strategies, like SEO, social media marketing, email marketing, and networking, to expand your reach and attract more potential customers.

CHAPTER 3: **YOUR PASSION YOUR NICHE**

Alright, my friend, it's time to talk about one of the most crucial aspects of affiliate marketing: finding your niche. The importance of choosing the right niche cannot be overstated. It's the foundation of your entire affiliate marketing business, and it's what will fuel your motivation, creativity, and, ultimately, your success.

So, what exactly is a niche? In simple terms, a niche is a specific segment of a market or industry that caters to a particular group of people with shared interests and needs. In the context of affiliate marketing, your niche is the area you'll focus on, create content around, and promote products or services within.

Now, let's dive into some essential tips for finding the perfect niche for your affiliate marketing journey:

- Follow Your Passion: When it comes to choosing a niche, passion is everything. Why? Because when you're genuinely excited and knowledgeable about a topic, it shows. Your enthusiasm will shine through your content, making it more engaging, authentic, and valuable to your audience. Plus, working on something you love makes the entire process much more enjoyable and sustainable in the long run.

- Evaluate the Market: While passion is essential, it's also important to consider the market demand and competition within your chosen niche. Ideally, you want to find a niche that has a sizable audience interested in the topic and a reasonable level of competition. This will ensure that there's enough demand for the products or services you'll be promoting while still giving you room to stand out and make an impact.

- Identify the Problems: One of the keys to affiliate marketing success is providing value and solving problems for your audience. So, when choosing your niche, think about the common issues, pain points, or challenges that people within that niche face. By identifying these problems, you'll be better equipped to create content and promote products that genuinely help your audience, ultimately leading to more sales and commissions.

- Assess the Monetization Potential: Lastly, consider the monetization potential of your chosen niche. Are there high-quality products or services available for promotion within the niche? Are there reputable affiliate programs or networks that cater to your niche? Evaluating the monetization opportunities is crucial to ensure that your affiliate marketing efforts can be profitable and worthwhile.

To sum it up, finding the perfect niche is all about striking the right balance between passion, market demand, problem-solving, and monetization potential. It may take some research, self-reflection, and trial and error, but trust me, it's worth the effort. Once you've found your sweet spot, you'll be well on your way to crushing it in the world of affiliate marketing. In the next chapter, we'll dive into the exciting process of building your online empire, creating a platform that showcases your expertise, and connecting with your target audience. Let's keep this momentum going, and remember – the hustle never stops!

CHAPTER 4: **BUILDING YOUR EMPIRE**

Now that you've chosen your niche and laid the foundation, it's time to start building your online empire. In this chapter, we'll dive into the importance of creating a strong online presence, using various platforms to connect with your target audience, and crafting a brand that truly resonates.

Creating an online presence is all about showcasing your expertise, building trust with your audience, and making it easy for people to find and connect with you. Your online presence is your digital storefront, and it's where you'll showcase your content, promote your affiliate offers, and cultivate a community of loyal followers and customers.

Here are some essential tips for building a killer online presence:

- Choose Your Platform: The first step in building your online presence is to choose the right platform(s) for your content. This could be a blog, a YouTube channel, a podcast, or social media platforms like Instagram, Facebook, or TikTok. When choosing your platform, consider your strengths, interests, and where your target audience is most likely to be found. It's also a good idea to diversify your presence across multiple platforms, as this can help you reach a wider audience and create multiple touchpoints for engagement.
- Create a Consistent Brand: Your brand is what sets you apart from the competition and makes you memorable to your audience. When building your online presence, focus on creating a consistent brand across all your platforms. This includes your logo, color scheme, typography, tone of voice, and overall aesthetic. A strong, consistent brand will help you build trust, recognition,

and authority within your niche. Your name can also be your brand and this is what I suggest.

- Optimize for SEO: One of the keys to a strong online presence is making sure people can find you easily through search engines like Google. This is where search engine optimization (SEO) comes into play. By optimizing your website, blog, or other content platforms for SEO, you can improve your visibility, drive organic traffic, and attract more potential customers to your affiliate offers, but don't worry about this for now. It's your next step.

- Engage with Your Audience: Building a successful online presence is not just about creating content – it's also about engaging with your audience and fostering a sense of community. Make sure to respond to comments, answer questions, and interact with your followers on social media. By doing so, you'll create a loyal and engaged audience that's more likely to trust your recommendations and convert into customers.

- Be Authentic and Transparent: In the world of affiliate marketing, trust is everything. To build trust with your audience, it's essential to be authentic, transparent, and genuine in your content and interactions. Don't try to be someone you're not, and don't promote products or services you don't genuinely believe in. By being true to yourself and your audience, you'll cultivate a loyal following that respects and values your recommendations.

By following these tips and putting in the hard work, you'll create a powerful online presence that sets the stage for affiliate marketing success. In the next chapter, we'll dive into the art of crafting high-quality, engaging content that keeps your audience coming back for more. Get ready to unleash your creativity and make your mark on the digital world!

CHAPTER 5: **CONTENT IS KING**

We've made it to one of the most critical aspects of affiliate marketing success: content creation. As the saying goes, "Content is King", and for a good reason. Your content is the vehicle through which you'll educate, entertain, engage, and ultimately, sell to your audience. Without high-quality content, even the best affiliate offers and promotional strategies will fall flat.

So, let's explore some essential tips for crafting killer content that keeps your audience coming back for more:

- Know Your Audience: Before you create any content, it's crucial to know your audience inside and out. Understand their needs, desires, pain points, and preferences. This will help you create content that genuinely resonates with them, addresses their concerns, and offers solutions to their problems.

- Be Valuable: Your content should provide value to your audience, whether it's through education, entertainment, inspiration, or problem-solving. Focus on delivering value first and foremost, and the sales will follow. Remember, people are more likely to trust and buy from someone who has already helped them in some way.

- Be Consistent: Consistency is key when it comes to content creation. Establish a regular posting schedule and stick to it as much as possible. This will help you stay top of mind with your audience, build trust, and keep your content fresh and relevant.

- Diversify Your Content: Don't be afraid to mix it up and experiment with different types of content, such as blog posts, videos, podcasts, infographics, or social media posts. Diversifying your content not only keeps things interesting for your audience but also allows you to reach and engage with different segments of your target market.

- Incorporate Storytelling: Storytelling is a powerful tool for creating engaging, memorable content. By sharing your personal experiences, lessons, and insights, you can connect with your audience on a deeper level and build a stronger emotional connection. Plus, stories are much easier to remember and share than dry facts or statistics.

- Optimize for Engagement: Encourage interaction and engagement with your content by asking questions, soliciting feedback, or incorporating calls-to-action (CTAs). This not only helps build a sense of community but also provides valuable insights into your audience's thoughts, opinions, and preferences.

- Track Your Performance: Finally, keep an eye on your content's performance and make data-driven decisions to optimize and improve. Use analytics tools to track key metrics like views, engagement, shares, and conversions. This will help you identify what's working, what's not, and where to focus your efforts moving forward.

By following these tips and consistently creating high-quality, engaging content, you'll establish yourself as an authority within your niche and cultivate a loyal, engaged audience that's more likely to convert into customers. In the next chapter, we'll dive into the art and science of promoting your affiliate offers and driving traffic to your content. Get ready to level up your marketing game and skyrocket your affiliate commissions!

CHAPTER 6: FINDING HIGH-TICKET OFFERS

In the world of affiliate marketing, promoting high-ticket offers can be a game-changer. These offers provide you with the opportunity to earn higher commissions per sale, which can lead to a more significant income stream. In this chapter, we'll explore how to find high-ticket affiliate marketing offers that align with your niche and audience.

- Research your niche: Before you can start promoting high-ticket offers, you need to understand your niche inside and out. Make a list of popular products or services that your target audience is interested in and that have higher price tags. This will give you a solid foundation for finding high-ticket affiliate programs.

- Use affiliate networks: Affiliate networks like ClickBank, CJ Affiliate, and ShareASale are excellent resources for discovering high-ticket offers. Search their platforms for products or services that match your niche and have a high commission rate. Keep an eye out for recurring commissions, as they can lead to long-term income.

- Visit company websites: Many companies offer affiliate programs directly through their websites. Browse the websites of popular brands within your niche to see if they have an affiliate program. Look for information about commission rates and any specific high-ticket products or services they offer.

- Join industry forums and communities: Engaging in online forums and communities related to your niche can provide invaluable insights into high-ticket offers. These spaces are often filled with experienced marketers who share their successes and recommend specific affiliate programs. Be sure to participate actively in these communities to build relationships and gain access to insider knowledge.

- Check out competitor websites: Keep an eye on your competitors and see what high-ticket offers they're promoting. This can give you an idea of what's working for others in your niche and help you identify potential opportunities for your own affiliate marketing business.

- Reach out to companies: If you've found a high-ticket product or service that you'd like to promote but can't find an affiliate program, don't be afraid to reach out to the company directly. They may have a private affiliate program or be open to creating one if they see the value in partnering with you.

- Be selective: When choosing high-ticket affiliate offers, prioritize quality over quantity. Promoting high-quality products or services that resonate with your audience will lead to higher conversion rates and a more sustainable income stream.

By following these steps, you'll be well on your way to finding high-ticket affiliate marketing offers that can boost your income and help you achieve financial freedom. Remember, success in affiliate marketing requires patience and persistence, so stay committed to your goals and continue refining your strategies as you grow.

CHAPTER 7: **TRAFFIC-DRIVING STRATEGIES**

You've built your online presence, crafted high-quality content, and carefully chosen your affiliate offers – now it's time to promote them and drive traffic to your platform. In this chapter, we'll explore various traffic-driving strategies that can help you reach more potential customers, boost engagement, and ultimately, increase your affiliate commissions.

- Master Social Media Marketing: Social media platforms like Facebook, Instagram, Twitter, and TikTok are powerful tools for promoting your content and affiliate offers. Develop a consistent posting schedule, share valuable content, engage with your audience, and leverage advertising options to expand your reach and drive targeted traffic to your platform.

- Leverage SEO: As mentioned earlier, search engine optimization (SEO) is crucial for driving organic traffic to your website, blog, or other content platforms. By optimizing your content for relevant keywords, improving your site's technical performance, and building high-quality backlinks, you can increase your visibility in search engine results and attract more potential customers.

- Utilize Email Marketing: Building an email list and leveraging email marketing is a highly effective way to keep your audience engaged, promote your content, and drive sales. Use lead magnets and opt-in forms to capture email addresses, and craft compelling email campaigns that deliver value, build trust, and promote your affiliate offers in a non-spammy way.

- Network and Collaborate: Connect with other influencers, bloggers, or content creators within your niche to expand your reach and tap into new audiences.

Collaborate on guest posts, podcasts, YouTube videos, or social media takeovers to gain exposure and drive traffic back to your platform. Remember, collaboration over competition is key to success in the online space.

- Invest in Paid Advertising: While organic strategies are essential, paid advertising can be a powerful way to drive targeted traffic to your content and affiliate offers. Platforms like Google Ads, Facebook Ads, and Instagram Ads allow you to reach specific audience segments with highly targeted campaigns, helping you maximize your return on investment.

- Optimize for Conversions: Finally, ensure that your platform is optimized for conversions by making it easy for visitors to find and act on your affiliate offers. This includes placing CTAs strategically throughout your content, using attention-grabbing visuals, and testing different elements like headlines, copy, and button colors to find what works best.

By implementing these traffic-driving strategies and continuously optimizing your efforts, you'll be well on your way to boosting your affiliate commissions and achieving success in the world of affiliate marketing. In the next chapter, we'll talk about some essential mindset shifts and success habits that'll help you stay motivated, focused, and on track for long-term affiliate marketing success. Let's finish strong and make your dreams a reality!

CHAPTER 8: MINDSET SHIFTS AND SUCCESS HABITS

Success in affiliate marketing – or any entrepreneurial venture, for that matter – is about more than just the strategies, tactics, and techniques. It's also about your mindset, habits, and approach to the journey. In this chapter, we'll explore some essential mindset shifts and success habits that'll help you stay motivated, focused, and on track for long-term affiliate marketing mastery.

- Embrace the Learning Curve: Affiliate marketing can be challenging, and there's always something new to learn. Embrace the learning process and view every challenge or obstacle as an opportunity to grow and improve. Remember, mastery takes time, so be patient with yourself and enjoy the journey.

- Develop a Growth Mindset: A growth mindset is a belief that your abilities, intelligence, and skills can be developed through dedication, effort, and perseverance. By adopting a growth mindset, you'll be more open to learning, experimentation, and embracing failure as a necessary part of growth.

- Set SMART Goals: Clearly defined goals are essential for staying focused and motivated in your affiliate marketing journey. Set SMART (Specific, Measurable, Achievable, Relevant, and Time-bound) goals for your business, and regularly review and adjust them as needed.

- Prioritize Time Management: Time is your most valuable resource, so make it a priority to manage it effectively. Develop a daily routine, break tasks into manageable chunks, and use productivity tools to help you stay organized and on track. Make sure you get rid of your hardest tasks in the morning, so you don't have to worry about them during the day.

- Network and Build Relationships: Success in affiliate marketing often comes down to the relationships you build within your niche and the online space. Actively network, collaborate and engage with others to expand your reach, learn from their experiences, and grow your business.

- Stay Consistent: Consistency is the key to building momentum, trust, and authority in your niche. Stick to your content schedule, maintain your online presence, and keep pushing forward, even when the going gets tough.

- Keep Adapting: The digital landscape is constantly evolving, and so should your approach to affiliate marketing. Stay informed about industry trends, new strategies, and emerging platforms, and be willing to adapt and pivot as needed to stay ahead of the game.

- Practice Gratitude and Celebrate Wins: Finally, take the time to practice gratitude and celebrate your wins, big and small. Acknowledging your accomplishments and expressing gratitude for your progress will help you stay motivated, inspired, and focused on the bigger picture.

By adopting these mindset shifts and success habits, you'll be well-equipped to navigate the ups and downs of the affiliate marketing journey and ultimately achieve the financial freedom and success you desire. Now, it's time to take action, put these strategies and principles into practice, and make your affiliate marketing dreams a reality. Remember, the only limit to your success is the one you set for yourself – so dream big, work hard, and never give up.

CHAPTER 9: SCALING YOUR BUSINESS

You've laid a solid foundation, you've learned how to build an engaged audience and started generating income through affiliate marketing. Now, it's time to take your business to the next level and scale it for even greater success. In this chapter, we'll explore strategies and tactics for scaling your affiliate marketing business and maximizing your earning potential.

- Diversify Your Affiliate Portfolio: One key to scaling your business is to diversify your affiliate portfolio by promoting multiple products, services, and programs. This not only helps you reach a broader audience but also mitigates the risk of relying on a single income source. Look for complementary offers within your niche that provide value to your audience and align with your brand.

- Create and Sell Your Own Products: While affiliate marketing can be incredibly lucrative, creating and selling your own products or services can help you scale your income even further. Consider developing digital products like e-books, courses, or workshops that address the needs and pain points of your audience. By offering your own products, you'll gain more control over your revenue and have the opportunity to create a more diverse and sustainable business model.

- Implement Advanced Marketing Strategies: As your business grows, it's essential to continually refine and expand your marketing strategies. Experiment with advanced tactics like retargeting ads, influencer partnerships, webinars, and content syndication to reach new audiences and boost your conversions.

- Automate and Delegate: Scaling your business requires efficient systems and processes to handle the increased workload. Automate tasks where possible, using tools like email autoresponders, social media schedulers, and CRM systems to streamline your operations. Additionally, consider outsourcing tasks or hiring a team to help you manage and grow your business more effectively. Great tool to automate your email campaigns is Notifao.

- Continuously Optimize Your Funnel: A well-optimized sales funnel is crucial for maximizing your conversions and revenue. Regularly test and tweak various elements of your funnel, such as your lead magnets, landing pages, email sequences, and CTAs, to identify areas for improvement and boost your overall performance. I highly recommend Notifao, as your sales funnel partner. Notifao also allows you to earn commission as its affiliate!

- Build Strategic Partnerships: Forming strategic partnerships with other businesses, influencers, or content creators in your niche can help you expand your reach, access new markets, and grow your business more quickly. Look for partners who share your values and target audience, and explore opportunities for collaboration, cross-promotion, or joint ventures.

- Invest in Personal and Professional Development: Finally, never stop investing in yourself and your growth as an entrepreneur. Attend industry conferences, join mastermind groups, and seek out mentorship opportunities to continually learn, grow, and stay ahead of the curve in your niche.

By implementing these strategies and focusing on continuous improvement, you'll be well on your way to scaling your affiliate marketing business and achieving even greater success. Remember, the sky's the limit – so keep dreaming big, pushing your boundaries, and reaching for new heights.

CHAPTER 10: BUILDING A COMMUNITY

In the world of affiliate marketing, building a community of loyal followers and customers is essential to long-term success. A strong, engaged community not only helps drive consistent traffic and conversions but also fosters trust, credibility, and authority within your niche. In this chapter, we'll explore strategies for cultivating loyalty and trust among your audience and turning them into a thriving community of supporters.

- Engage with Your Audience: To build a strong community, it's crucial to engage with your audience regularly. Respond to comments, answer questions, and participate in conversations across your blog, social media platforms, and other channels. Show your audience that you genuinely care about them and are invested in their success.

- Share Your Journey: People love to follow and support someone who's authentic and relatable. Share your personal journey, challenges, and victories within the affiliate marketing space. By being open and transparent, you'll create a deeper connection with your audience and inspire them to join you on your path to success.

- Provide Value Consistently: Consistently delivering valuable content is key to building trust and loyalty among your audience. Focus on addressing their needs, pain points, and desires through high-quality content, and always strive to overdeliver in terms of value.

- Create a Safe and Supportive Space: Encourage open communication, collaboration, and support within your community. Create a safe and inclusive space where members feel comfortable sharing their experiences, asking questions, and offering advice. This can be done through platforms like Facebook groups, online forums, or even live events.

- Offer Exclusive Benefits: Reward your loyal followers with exclusive benefits, such as access to premium content, discounts on products or services, or priority support. This not only helps to nurture loyalty and trust but also encourages more people to join your community and become engaged members.

- Encourage User-Generated Content: User-generated content (UGC), such as testimonials, reviews, or social media posts, is a powerful way to build trust and showcase the success of your audience members. Encourage your community to share their experiences, results, and insights, and highlight their achievements to inspire and motivate others.

- Celebrate Community Milestones: Lastly, celebrate your community's milestones and achievements, such as reaching a specific number of followers, hitting revenue targets, or completing challenges. This not only fosters a sense of unity and camaraderie but also keeps your community engaged and motivated to continue supporting you and each other.

By focusing on building a loyal and engaged community, you'll lay the foundation for long-term success in your affiliate marketing business. Remember, your community is your greatest asset – so nurture it, invest in it, and watch it grow alongside your business.

CHAPTER 11: BUILDING PASSIVE INCOME

One of the best aspects of affiliate marketing is its potential for passive income. By setting up systems that continue to generate revenue even when you're not actively working, you can create a steady stream of income that keeps coming.

- To do this, start by focusing on evergreen content. This type of content remains relevant and valuable over time, attracting traffic and generating sales long after it's been published. Examples include how-to guides, tutorials, and product reviews. By creating high-quality evergreen content, you'll build a foundation that continues to bring in income.

- Next, automate your marketing efforts where possible. Use email marketing platforms to set up automated email sequences that nurture leads and promote affiliate products. Utilize social media scheduling tools to consistently share content and engage with your audience. Again, Notifao will be helpful.

- Finally, diversify your income sources. Don't rely solely on one product, platform, or traffic source. By building multiple streams of income, you'll reduce the risk of losing everything if one of them fails. As you continue to grow your affiliate marketing business, explore new opportunities and expand your portfolio of income sources.

CHAPTER 12: EVOLVING WITH THE INDUSTRY

The world of affiliate marketing is constantly changing, and to stay successful, you must be willing to evolve with it. By staying informed about industry trends and adapting your strategies accordingly, you'll ensure your affiliate marketing business remains sustainable and profitable.

- First, make a habit of regularly consuming content related to affiliate marketing. Subscribe to newsletters, listen to podcasts, and follow industry leaders on social media. This will help you stay up-to-date on the latest trends, tools, and tactics.

- Second, always be open to learning and trying new strategies. What works today might not work tomorrow, so be prepared to adapt your approach as needed. Experiment with different tactics, analyze the results and adjust your plan based on what's working and what's not.

- Lastly, invest in your personal and professional development. Attend conferences, take online courses, and network with other affiliate marketers. By constantly learning and growing, you'll be better equipped to navigate the ever-changing world of affiliate marketing and maintain long-term success.

CHAPTER 13: **LONG-TERM SUCCESS**

Achieving long-term success in the affiliate marketing space requires dedication, persistence, and the ability to adapt to an ever-changing digital landscape. In this final chapter, we'll discuss strategies for maintaining your momentum and staying committed to your business for years to come.

- Set Long-Term Goals: Establish long-term goals for your affiliate marketing business that align with your values, passions, and overall vision. These goals will serve as a guiding light, keeping you focused and motivated during challenging times.

- Embrace Change and Innovation: The digital marketing landscape is constantly evolving, and successful affiliate marketers must be willing to embrace change and adapt their strategies accordingly. Stay informed about industry trends, emerging platforms, and new marketing techniques to stay ahead of the curve and maintain your competitive edge.

- Prioritize Self-Care and Work-Life Balance: As an entrepreneur, it's crucial to prioritize self-care and maintain a healthy work-life balance. By taking care of your physical, mental, and emotional well-being, you'll be better equipped to face challenges, make informed decisions, and remain dedicated to your business over the long haul.

- Continuously Learn and Grow: Commit to lifelong learning and personal development by regularly investing in courses, books, seminars, and mentorship opportunities. As you grow and evolve, so will your business.

- Monitor and Analyze Your Performance: Regularly track

and analyze your business's performance to identify areas for improvement, capitalize on opportunities, and make data-driven decisions. By staying proactive and responsive, you'll be better equipped to navigate the ups and downs of the affiliate marketing journey.

- Stay Connected to Your Community: Don't underestimate the power of a strong support network. Stay connected to your community of fellow entrepreneurs, mentors, and industry professionals to share ideas, seek guidance, and collaborate on new opportunities.

- Keep Challenging Yourself: As you achieve success in your affiliate marketing business, don't become complacent. Continuously challenge yourself to set new goals, explore new strategies, and push the boundaries of what's possible in your niche.

By staying committed, adaptable, and focused on continuous growth, you'll be well-prepared to navigate the ever-changing world of affiliate marketing and achieve long-term success.

We've covered a comprehensive range of topics, and with this knowledge, you're now equipped to embark on your affiliate marketing journey and build a thriving, sustainable business. Remember, success in affiliate marketing is a marathon, not a sprint. Stay patient, persistent, and dedicated to your vision, and you'll be well on your way to achieving the financial freedom and lifestyle you've always dreamed of. Good luck, and go make your mark on the world!

Success is all about taking action. Don't just consume this e-book – go out there and make your mark on the world. I'm rooting for you! Let's crush it!

Paul Wu